Chasing Dreams
For String Orchestra

Xavier Hersom

Copyright © 2022 Xavier Hersom. All rights reserved.
Photography by Marti Steiner Unger
ISMN 979-0-60028-007-0
ISBN-13: 978-1-7376602-6-2
For more information, please visit: www.XavierHersom.com

For public performance permission, contact Xavier Hersom at:

XavierHersomMusic@gmail.com

For bulk orders, go to www.XavierHersom.com

This piece is dedicated to all students and educators who experienced depression during the COVID-19 pandemic, yet still managed to chase their dreams and inspire others.

CONTENTS

Program Note

Performance Note

Score

Violin I

Violin II

Viola

Cello

Double Bass

Recording Link

About the Composer

Program Note

"Chasing Dreams" is a highly emotional piece about the journey of achieving one's dream despite adversity. It is dedicated to all students and educators who experienced depression during the COVID-19 pandemic, yet still managed to chase their dreams and inspire others.

Performance Note

"Chasing Dreams" is well suited for a collegiate concert or graduation ceremony. Ideally this piece would be performed by a large string orchestra to accentuate the contrast between solo and tutti. While "Chasing Dreams" is open to some interpretation, the following context about the titled sections should be considered as a guide for performance: "Fantasy" should sound wistful as a daydream developing in clarity. "The Dream is a Reality!" is the first time all instruments come together (tutti), and it should be a powerful statement. The imitation of "Supporting Friendships" symbolizes how interwoven relationships make life beautiful. "Ambition" should be steady with passion. "The Chase!" is the climax of the piece and should be very spirited—particularly for violin I. "Never Give Up" starts with lower strings transitioning to G major then rises to the highest note in the piece (high D in violin I)—this is supposed to sound like reaching the peak of a mountain. "Reflection" is looking down on the valley and taking pride in the journey. "Finale" signifies the triumph of reaching the end of the pursuit.

Duration: ca. 4' 30"

Grade 4

Score

Score
Chasing Dreams
Xavier Hersom

Dedicated to students and educators who experienced depression during COVID-19,
yet still managed to follow their dreams and inspire others.

©2022

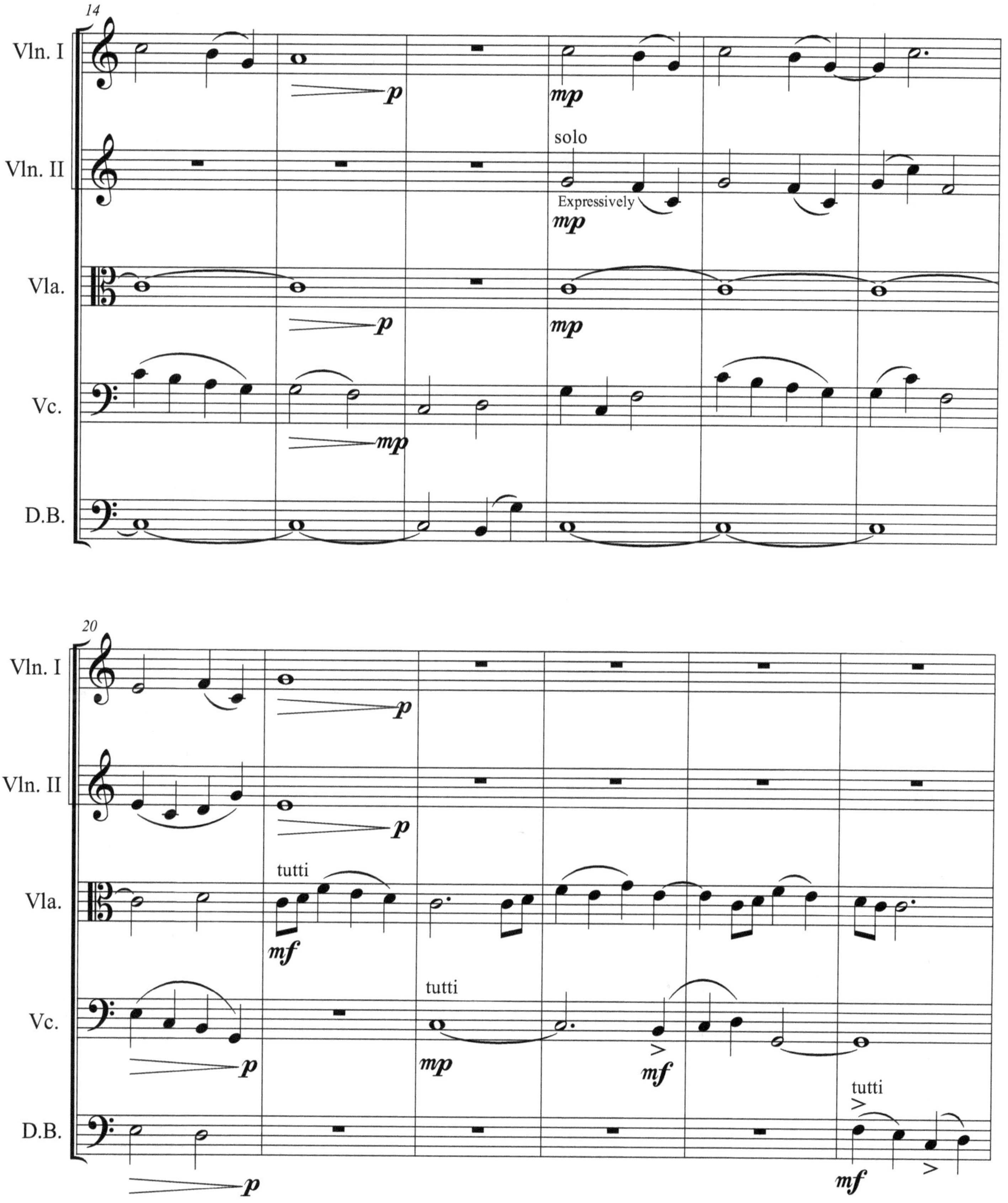
14
Vln. I
Vln. II
Vla.
Vc.
D.B.
p
mp
solo
Expressively
mp
p
mp
mp
20
Vln. I
Vln. II
Vla.
Vc.
D.B.
p
p
tutti
mf
tutti
mp
mf
p
tutti
p
mf

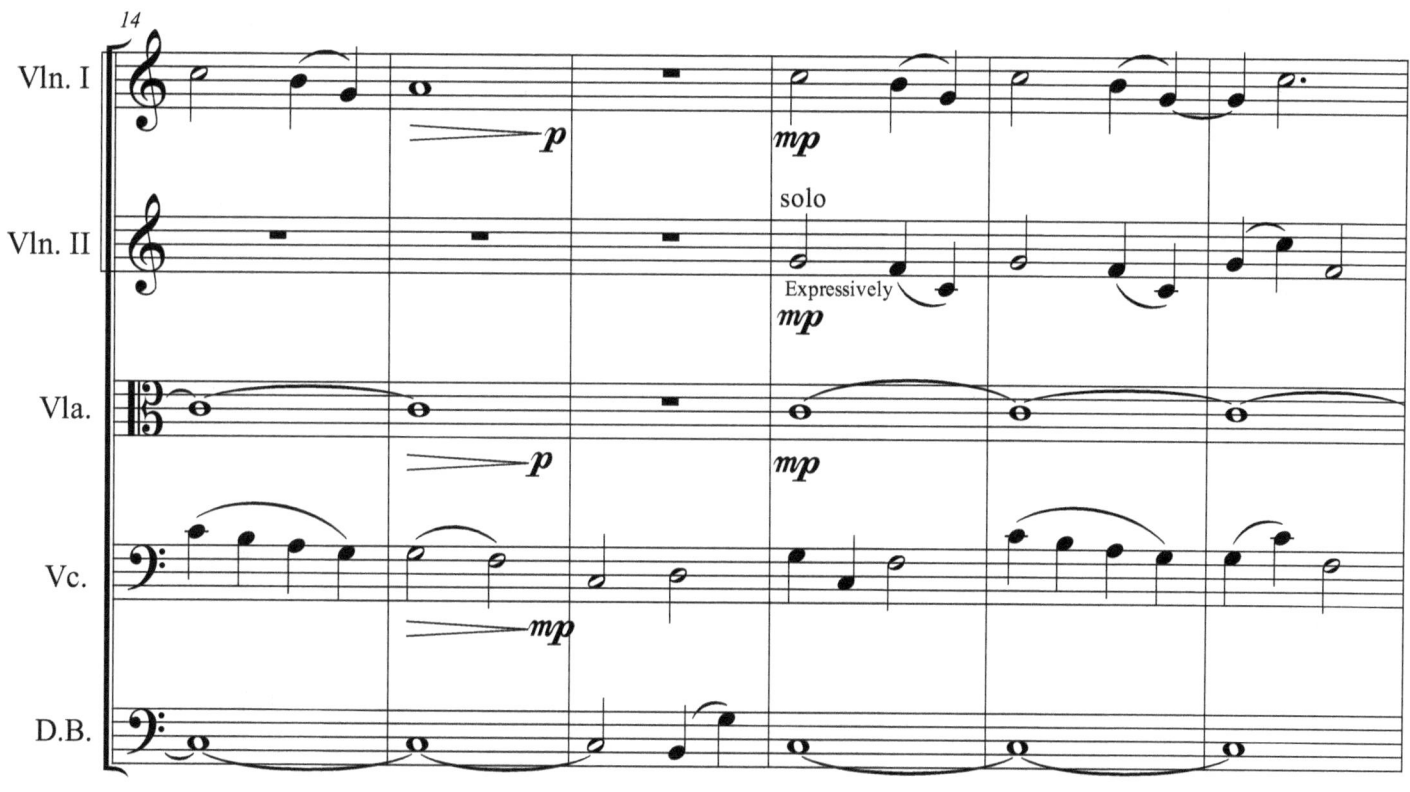

Chasing Dreams

3

Chasing Dreams

Violin I

Violin II

Chasing Dreams

Viola

Viola

Chasing Dreams

Xavier Hersom

Dedicated to students and educators who experienced depression during COVID-19,
yet still managed to follow their dreams and inspire others.

©2022

Chasing Dreams

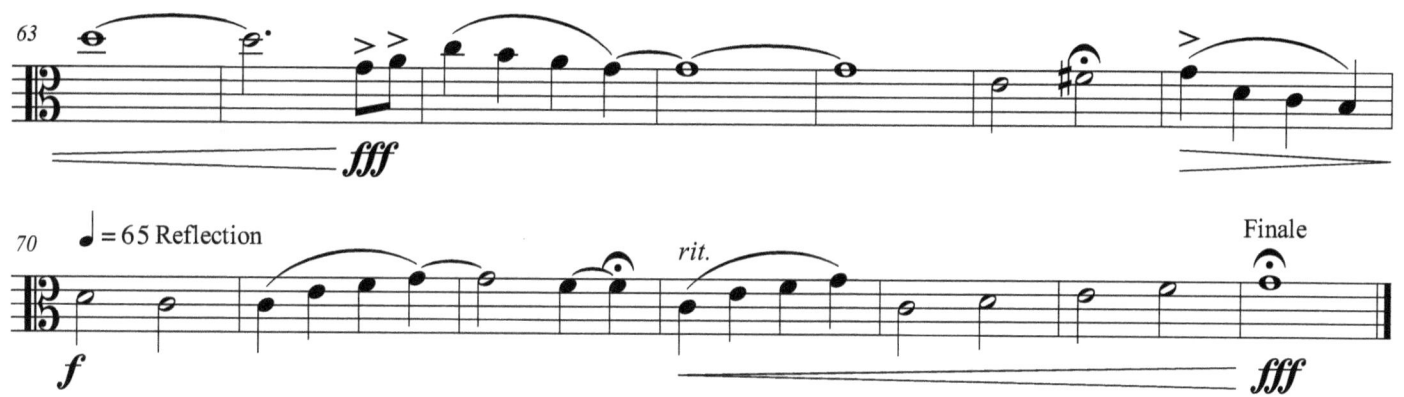

Cello

Cello — **Chasing Dreams** — Xavier Hersom

Dedicated to students and educators who experienced depression during COVID-19,
yet still managed to follow their dreams and inspire others.

©2022

Double Bass

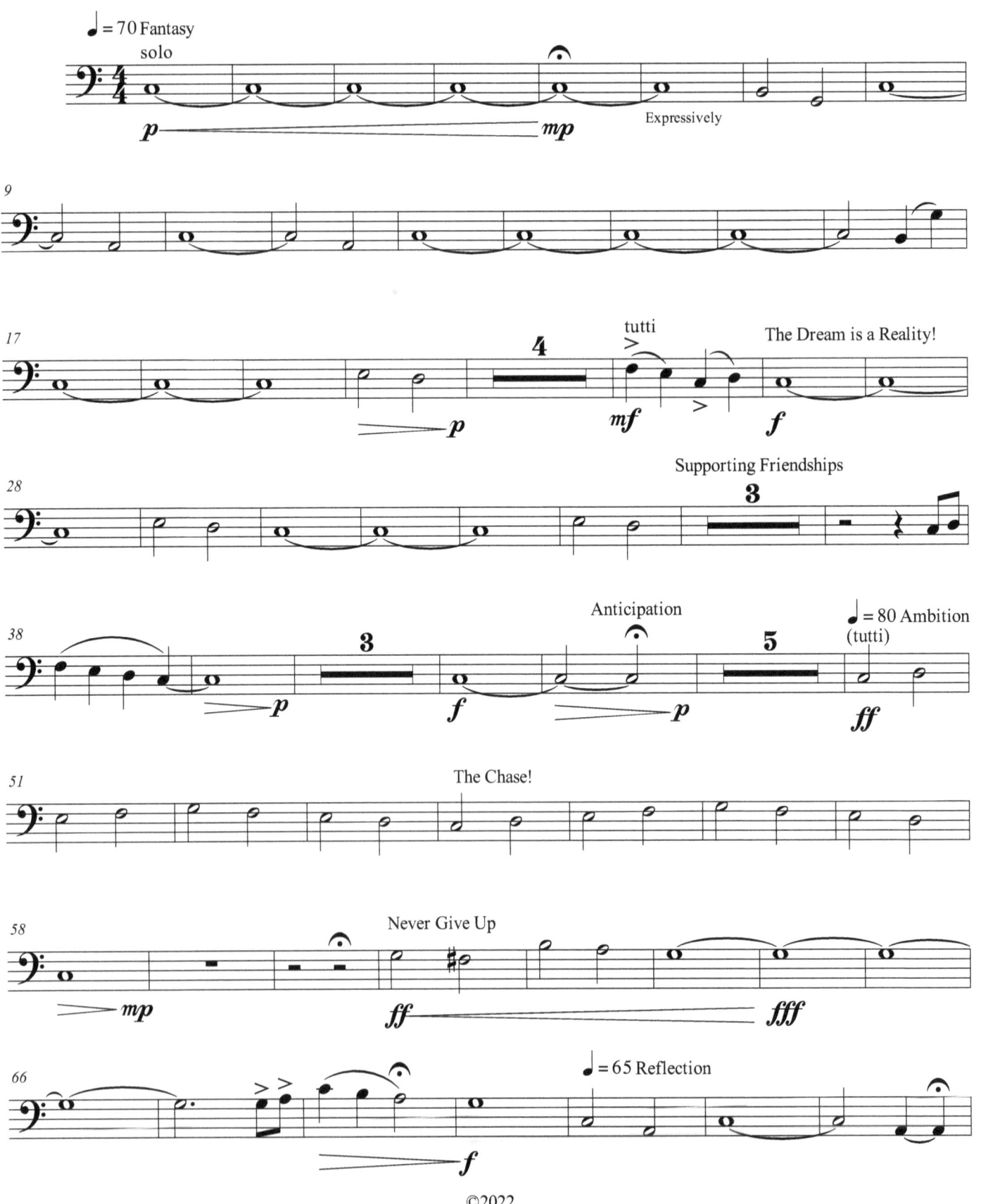

Listen to a recording here:

About the Composer

Xavier Hersom (b.1995) is an international-award-winning American composer. Though influenced by tonal music of the Romantic period, Hersom's compositions are inspired by current national issues. He believes art enables people to see the world from other perspectives and that music can spread awareness of social injustices. Learn more about him at:

www.XavierHersom.com

If you enjoy this music, please consider leaving a review.

Thank you!

www.ingramcontent.com/pod-product-compliance
Lightning Source LLC
Chambersburg PA
CBHW080351170426
43194CB00014B/2751